BinaryCoder X

Programming Languages and how to use them

"Dedicated to the relentless spirit of every coder - the architects of the digital realm. May your keystrokes be bold, your logic flawless, and your creations illuminate the vast expanse of the programming cosmos. Happy coding to all the dreamers and builders shaping the future, one line at a time."

"Uncover the poetry in every line of code, as BinaryCoder X invites you to dance with programming languages. In this symphony of logic and creativity, embark on a journey where every keystroke echoes the artistry of digital creation. Welcome to 'Programming Languages and How to Use Them' — where innovation meets expression, and your code becomes the brushstroke painting the canvas of technology."

BinaryCoder X

Contents

1.

2.

3.

4.

5.

6.

7.

8.

9.

10.

11.

12.

13.

14.

15.

16.

17.

18.

19.

20.

21.

22.

23.

24.

25.

26.

27.

28.

29.

30.

31.

32.

Foreword

Foreword

In the dynamic world of technology, where the only constant is change, the ability to communicate with machines through programming languages is an indispensable skill. "Programming Languages and How to Use Them" by BinaryCoder X is not just a book; it's a key that unlocks the door to a realm where lines of code become the architects of our digital future.

In these pages, BinaryCoder X, a maestro in the symphony of binaries and algorithms, shares profound insights into the languages that drive innovation, power applications, and shape the digital landscape. The journey through this book is an immersive experience, traversing the vibrant syntax of languages such as Python, JavaScript, Java, and beyond.

As you embark on this odyssey, you'll find not just code snippets but a narrative that demystifies the nuances of each language. BinaryCoder X is not just a guide but a storyteller, weaving tales of creativity, problem-solving, and the boundless potential encoded in every line.

This book is a testament to the universality of programming. Whether you're a student taking your first steps, a seasoned developer seeking mastery, or an enthusiast driven by curiosity, BinaryCoder X provides a roadmap through the rich tapestry of programming languages.

Remember, this is not a static manual but a living testament to the ever-evolving landscape of technology. Each language introduced by BinaryCoder X is a tool waiting to be wielded, a palette waiting for your creative strokes.

So, dive in. Immerse yourself in the syntax, savor the challenges, and let BinaryCoder X be your guide through the fascinating world of programming languages. As you navigate through these pages, may you not only learn the languages but also discover the artistry, the passion, and the limitless possibilities that await when you speak the language of machines.

Happy coding!

BinaryCoder   X

Preface

Preface

Welcome to the exciting world of programming languages, a realm where creativity meets logic, and ideas transform into powerful lines of code. In "Programming Languages and How to Use Them" by BinaryCoder X, embark on a journey that demystifies the languages shaping our digital landscape.

As technology evolves, the importance of programming languages becomes increasingly evident. Whether you're a novice exploring the wonders of coding or a seasoned developer seeking new perspectives, this book serves as your compass through the diverse landscape of programming languages.

BinaryCoder X, an entity immersed in the binary fabric of digital realms, guides you through the intricacies of languages like Python, JavaScript, Java, C#, and beyond. Each chapter unveils the unique characteristics and applications of a programming language, offering hands-on insights into writing, compiling, and running code.

From the elegant simplicity of Python to the efficiency of C++ and the functional beauty of Haskell, you'll discover the language that resonates with your coding style. The prelude of each language provides a glimpse into its syntax, key features, and real-world applications, ensuring a holistic understanding.

This book is not merely a manual but an invitation to explore the artistry within programming. BinaryCoder X encourages you to experiment, learn, and break through the confines of your comfort zone. Whether you're scripting dynamic web applications, optimizing algorithms, or diving into the depths of data science, each chapter equips you with the tools to navigate the programming landscape.

As BinaryCoder X takes you on this odyssey, remember that programming is not just about mastering languages; it's about crafting solutions, unraveling complexities, and embracing the ever-changing canvas of technology. So, let the journey begin, and may your code echo in the binary symphony of innovation!

Happy coding!

BinaryCoder   X

Acknowledgement

Acknowledgments

Embarking on the journey of crafting "Programming Languages and How to Use Them" has been a thrilling odyssey, and this endeavor would not have been possible without the support, inspiration, and collective effort of many remarkable individuals.

To the coding community, whose vibrant spirit and tireless pursuit of innovation fuel the ever-evolving landscape of programming languages - you are the heartbeat of this book. Your passion for pushing boundaries and embracing the unknown inspires BinaryCoder X to delve deeper into the realms of code.

A heartfelt gratitude to mentors and educators, whose guidance forms the bedrock of knowledge. Your commitment to nurturing the next generation of coders is both admirable and pivotal in shaping the future of technology.

To the open-source contributors and the global coding community, thank you for fostering an environment of collaboration and shared learning. Your dedication to the collective advancement of technology is a beacon for aspiring coders worldwide.

A special nod to the pioneers and visionaries who laid the foundation for the diverse ecosystem of programming languages. Your groundbreaking work has paved the way for countless innovations and continues to shape the way we interact with technology.

To my family and friends, your unwavering support and encouragement have been the driving force behind the late-night coding sessions, the countless "aha" moments, and the triumphs over stubborn bugs. Thank you for being the pillars of strength throughout this coding expedition.

Last but certainly not least, to the readers of this book - thank you for embarking on this adventure with BinaryCoder X. May the pages ahead inspire and empower you to unravel the mysteries of programming languages and discover the boundless possibilities that coding affords.

Happy coding to all!

BinaryCoder   X

1

C#

To use C# (number 4 in the list of programming languages):

1. IDE: Install Visual Studio, a powerful IDE for C# development.

2. Write Code: Create a `.cs` file and write a simple C# program.

```csharp
   using System;

class Program {
    static void Main() {
    Console.WriteLine("Hello, World!");
    }
    }
```

3. Compile and Run: Visual Studio will handle compilation and execution for you.

4. Explore .NET: C# is commonly used with the .NET framework; explore ASP.NET for web development or Xamarin for mobile apps.

Happy coding with C#!

2

Python

To use Python (number 1 in the list of programming languages), follow these general steps:

1. Installation: Install Python on your computer. You can download it from the official Python website (https://www.python.org/).

2. Text Editor or IDE: Choose a text editor or an Integrated Development Environment (IDE) to write your Python code. Popular choices include Visual Studio Code, PyCharm, and Jupyter Notebooks.

3. Write Code: Open your chosen editor/IDE and start writing Python code. A simple "Hello, World!" program might look like this:

```python
   print("Hello, World!")
```

4. Run Code: Save your Python file with a `.py` extension (e.g., `hello.py`). Open a terminal or command prompt, navigate to the file's directory, and run the script:

```bash
   python hello.py
```

This will execute your Python code, and you should see the output.

5. Explore Python Libraries: Python has a rich ecosystem of libraries. Explore and use them for various tasks, such as NumPy for numerical operations, pandas for data manipulation, and Flask/Django for web development.

Remember, this is just a basic overview. As you progress, you can delve into more advanced topics and projects.

3

JavaScript

To use JavaScript (number 2 in the list of programming languages):

1. Text Editor: Choose a text editor like Visual Studio Code.

2. Write Code: Create a `.js` file, write your JavaScript code.

```javascript
   console.log("Hello, World!");
```

3. Run Code: Open the HTML file or run in a JavaScript environment.

4. Explore Libraries: Use frameworks like React or Node.js for specific tasks.

Keep it brief, and happy coding!

4

Java

To use Java (number 3 in the list of programming languages):

1. IDE: Install an Integrated Development Environment (IDE) like IntelliJ or Eclipse.

2. Write Code: Create a `.java` file and write a simple Java program.

```java
public class HelloWorld {
public static void main(String[] args) {
System.out.println("Hello, World!");
}
}
```

3. Compile: Use the IDE or run `javac HelloWorld.java` in the.

4. Run Code: Execute the compiled program with `java HelloWorld`.

5. Explore Frameworks: Java offers frameworks like Spring for web development.

Enjoy coding in Java!

5

C++

To use C++ (number 5 in the list of programming languages):

1. IDE: Install an Integrated Development Environment like Visual Studio or Code::Blocks.

2. Write Code: Create a `.cpp` file and write a simple C++ program.

```cpp
#include <iostream>

int main() {
    std::cout << "Hello, World!" << std::endl;
    return 0;
    }
```

3. Compile: Use a C++ compiler like g++ (`g++ -o HelloWorld HelloWorld.cpp`).

4. Run Code: Execute the compiled program (`./HelloWorld` in the terminal).

5. Explore STL: Learn and use the Standard Template Library (STL) for various data structures and algorithms.

Happy coding with C++!

6

Ruby

To use Ruby (number 6 in the list of programming languages):

1. Interpreter: Ruby is often interpreted. Make sure Ruby is installed on your system.

2. Write Code: Create a `.rb` file and write a simple Ruby program.

```ruby
puts "Hello, World!"
```

3. Run Code: Open a terminal, navigate to the file's directory, and run `ruby filename.rb`.

4. Explore Gems: Ruby's package manager, Gems, offers a variety of libraries. Explore and use them for different functionalities.

18

Enjoy coding in Ruby!

7

Swift

To use Swift (number 7 in the list of programming languages):

1. Xcode: Install Xcode, the official IDE for Swift development on macOS.

2. Write Code: Create a `.swift` file and write a simple Swift program.

```swift
print("Hello, World!")
```

3. Run Code: Use Xcode to build and run your Swift program.

4. Explore SwiftUI: For iOS/macOS app development, explore SwiftUI as a declarative framework.

Happy coding with Swift!

8

Kotlin

To use Kotlin (number 8 in the list of programming languages):

1. IDE: Install an Integrated Development Environment (IDE) like IntelliJ IDEA or Android Studio.

2. Write Code: Create a `.kt` file and write a simple Kotlin program.

```kotlin
fun main() {
println("Hello, World!")
}
```

3. Run Code: Use the IDE to run the Kotlin program.

4. Explore Android Development: Kotlin is widely used for Android app development. Consider exploring Android development using Kotlin.

22

Enjoy coding with Kotlin!

9

TypeScript

To use TypeScript (number 9 in the list of programming languages):

1. IDE: Use Visual Studio Code or any IDE that supports TypeScript.

2. Write Code: Create a `.ts` file and write TypeScript code.

```typescript
console.log("Hello, World!");
```

3. Compile: Use the TypeScript compiler (`tsc filename.ts`) to generate JavaScript.

4. Run Code: Execute the generated JavaScript file in a Node.js environment or include it in an HTML file for browser execution.

Explore TypeScript's static typing and modern features. Happy   coding!

10

PHP

To use PHP (number 10 in the list of programming languages):

1. Server Environment:Set up a server environment with PHP installed, or use a local server like XAMPP.

2. Write Code: Create a `.php` file and write a simple PHP script.

```php
<?php
echo "Hello, World!";
?>
```

3. Run Code: Place the file in the server's web directory and open it in a web browser.

4. Explore Frameworks: Explore PHP frameworks like Laravel for web development.

Happy coding with PHP!

11

Go

To use Go (number 11 in the list of programming languages):

1. Installation: Install Go on your machine. Set up your Go workspace.

2. Write Code: Create a `.go` file and write a simple Go program.

```go
    package main

import "fmt"

func main() {
    fmt.Println("Hello, World!")
    }
```

```

3. Run Code: Open a terminal, navigate to the file's directory, and run `go run filename.go`.

4. Explore Packages: Go has a powerful standard library. Explore and use packages for different functionalities.

Enjoy                    coding                    with                    Go!
```

12

Rust

To use Rust (number 12 in the list of programming languages):

1. Installation: Install Rust using the official installer from rustup.rs.

2. Write Code: Create a `.rs` file and write a simple Rust program.

```rust
fn main() {
println!("Hello, World!");
}
```

3. Compile and Run: Open a terminal, navigate to the file's directory, and run `cargo run` to compile and execute your Rust program.

4. Explore Ownership: Rust's ownership system is a unique feature. Explore and understand ownership, borrowing, and lifetimes.

Happy coding with Rust!

13

Objective-C

To use Objective-C (number 13 in the list of programming languages):

1. Xcode: Install Xcode, the official IDE for Objective-C development on macOS.

2. Write Code: Create a `.m` file and write a simple Objective-C program.

```objective-c
#import <Foundation/Foundation.h>

int main() {
    @autoreleasepool {
    NSLog(@"Hello, World!");
    }
    return 0;
```

```
}
```

3. Compile and Run: Use Xcode to compile and run your Objective-C program.

4. Explore Cocoa: Objective-C is commonly used with the Cocoa framework. Explore Cocoa for macOS and iOS app development.

Happy coding with Objective-C!

14

Chapter 14

To use Dart (number 14 in the list of programming languages):

1. **Installation:** Install Dart SDK from the official website (https://dart.dev/get-dart

2. **IDE:** Use an IDE like Visual Studio Code with the Dart plugi

3. **Write Code:** Create a `.dart` file and write a simple Dart progra

```da
  void main()
  print("Hello, World!")
```

`` `

4. Run Code: Open a terminal, navigate to the file's directory, and run `dart filename.dart

5. **Explore Flutter:** Dart is widely used with Flutter for cross-platform mobile app development. Consider exploring Flutter for building mobile application

Happy coding with Dart!lds.`.`};{rtm.n.).!ls.`.`};{rtm.n.). coding   with   Dart!

15

MATLAB

To use MATLAB (number 15 in the list of programming languages):

1. Installation: Install MATLAB on your machine.

2. MATLAB Environment:Open MATLAB and create a new script or function file.

3. Write Code: Write a simple MATLAB script.

```matlab
   disp('Hello, World!');
```

4. Run Code: Execute the script in the MATLAB environment.

5. Explore Simulink: MATLAB is often used with Simulink for simulation and model-based design. Explore Simulink for more advanced projects.

Happy coding with MATLAB!

16

R

To use R (number 16 in the list of programming languages):

1. Installation: Install R from the official CRAN website (https://cran.r-project.org/).

2. RStudio: Use RStudio, a popular IDE for R.

3. Write Code: Create an R script or RMarkdown document and write a simple R program.

```r
cat("Hello, World!\n")
```

4. Run Code: Execute the script in RStudio or through the R console.

5. Explore Data Analysis: R is widely used for data analysis and statistics. Explore packages like ggplot2 for data visualization and dplyr for data manipulation.

Happy coding with R!

17

Shell scripting

To use Shell scripting (number 17 in the list of programming languages):

1. Terminal: Open a terminal or command prompt on your system.

2. Write Code: Create a `.sh` file and write a simple Shell script.

```bash
#!/bin/bash
echo "Hello, World!"
```

3. Run Code: Make the script executable (`chmod +x filename.sh`) and execute it (`./filename.sh`).

4. Explore Unix Commands: Shell scripting is often used for automating tasks on Unix-like systems. Explore and use Unix commands within your scripts.

Happy coding with Shell scripting!

18

HTML/CSS

To work with HTML/CSS (number 18 in the list, though not programming languages but essential for web development):

1. Text Editor: Use a text editor like Visual Studio Code or Sublime Text.

2. Write Code:
   - For HTML, create an `.html` file and structure your document.

```html
<!DOCTYPE html>
<html>
<head>
<title>Hello, World!</title>
</head>
```

```html
<body>
<h1>Hello, World!</h1>
</body>
</html>
```

- For CSS, create a `.css` file and style your HTML.

```css
body {
background-color: #f0f0f0;
font-family: Arial, sans-serif;
}

h1 {
color: navy;
}
```

3. Preview Code: Open the HTML file in a web browser to see the result.

4. Explore Responsive Design: Learn about responsive design and CSS frameworks like Bootstrap for building responsive websites.

Happy coding with HTML and CSS!

19

Scala

To use Scala (number 19 in the list of programming languages):

1. IDE: Install an Integrated Development Environment (IDE) like IntelliJ IDEA with Scala plugin.

2. Write Code: Create a `.scala` file and write a simple Scala program.

```scala
object HelloWorld {
def main(args: Array[String]): Unit = {
println("Hello, World!")
}
}
```

3. Compile and Run: Use the IDE or run `scalac HelloWorld.scala` to compile and `scala HelloWorld` to execute.

4. Explore Akka and Play Framework: Scala is often used with Akka for concurrency and the Play Framework for web development.

Enjoy coding with Scala!

20

Groovy

To use Groovy (number 20 in the list of programming languages):

1. IDE: Use an Integrated Development Environment (IDE) like IntelliJ IDEA with Groovy support.

2. Write Code: Create a `.groovy` file and write a simple Groovy script.

```groovy
println "Hello, World!"
```

3. Run Code: Use the IDE or run `groovy filename.groovy` in the terminal.

4. Explore Grails: Groovy is often used with the Grails framework for web development. Explore Grails for building web applications.

Happy coding with Groovy!

21

Lua

To use Lua (number 21 in the list of programming languages):

1. Interpreter: Lua is often interpreted. Ensure Lua is installed on your system.

2. Write Code: Create a `.lua` file and write a simple Lua script.

```lua
print("Hello, World!")
```

3. Run Code: Open a terminal, navigate to the file's directory, and run `lua filename.lua` or use an online Lua interpreter.

4. Explore Embedded Systems: Lua is commonly used for embedded systems and game development. Explore Lua for scripting in various applications.

Enjoy coding with Lua!

22

Perl

To use Perl (number 22 in the list of programming languages):

1. Interpreter: Perl is often interpreted. Ensure Perl is installed on your system.

2. Write Code: Create a `.pl` file and write a simple Perl script.

```perl
   print "Hello, World!\n";
```

3. Run Code: Open a terminal, navigate to the file's directory, and run `perl filename.pl`.

4. Explore CPAN: Perl has a vast collection of modules on CPAN (Comprehensive Perl Archive Network). Explore and use CPAN modules for various tasks.

Happy coding with Perl!

23

Julia

To use Julia (number 23 in the list of programming languages):

1. IDE: Use an Integrated Development Environment (IDE) like VSCode with the Julia extension.

2. Write Code: Create a `.jl` file and write a simple Julia program.

```julia
    println("Hello, World!")
```

3. Run Code: Use the IDE or run `julia filename.jl` in the terminal.

4. Explore Data Science: Julia is known for its performance in scientific computing and data science. Explore packages like DataFrames.jl and Plots.jl.

Enjoy coding with Julia!

24

Haskell

To use Haskell (number 24 in the list of programming languages):

1. Compiler: Install the Glasgow Haskell Compiler (GHC) on your machine.

2. Write Code: Create a `.hs` file and write a simple Haskell program.

```haskell
main :: IO ()
main = putStrLn "Hello, World!"
```

3. Compile and Run: Open a terminal, navigate to the file's directory, and run `ghc filename.hs` to compile. Then execute the generated executable.

4. Explore Functional Programming: Haskell is a functional programming language. Explore concepts like pure functions, immutability, and monads.

Happy coding with Haskell!

25

F#

To use F# (number 25 in the list of programming languages):

1. IDE: Use an Integrated Development Environment (IDE) like Visual Studio or Visual Studio Code with F# support.

2. Write Code: Create an `.fs` file and write a simple F# program.

```fsharp
printfn "Hello, World!"
```

3. Compile and Run: Use the IDE or run `dotnet fsi filename.fsx` in the terminal.

4. Explore Functional-First Approach: F# is a functional-first language on the .NET platform. Explore functional programming concepts and integration with .NET libraries.

Enjoy coding with F#!

26

Assembly language

To use Assembly language (number 26 in the list of programming languages):

1. Assembler: Choose an assembler suitable for your target architecture.

2. Write Code: Create a `.asm` file and write assembly code.

```assembly
   section .data
   hello db 'Hello, World!', 0

section .text
   global _start

_start:
   ; write to stdout
```

```
    mov eax, 4
    mov ebx, 1
    mov ecx, hello
    mov edx, 13
    int 0x80

; exit
    mov eax, 1
    xor ebx, ebx
    int 0x80
```

3. Assemble and Run: Use the appropriate commands for your assembler and platform.

4. Explore Low-Level Programming: Assembly provides a close-to-hardware programming experience. Explore low-level concepts and system-level programming.

Happy coding with Assembly language!

27

COBOL

To use COBOL (number 27 in the list of programming languages):

1. Compiler: Install a COBOL compiler like GnuCOBOL.

2. Write Code: Create a `.cob` file and write a simple COBOL program.

```cobol
IDENTIFICATION DIVISION.
PROGRAM-ID. HelloWorld.

PROCEDURE DIVISION.
DISPLAY 'Hello, World!'.
STOP RUN.
```

3. Compile and Run: Use the appropriate commands for your COBOL compiler.

4. Explore Legacy Systems:COBOL is often used in legacy systems. Explore COBOL for maintaining or modernizing existing systems.

Happy   coding   with   COBOL!

28

Fortran

To use Fortran (number 28 in the list of programming languages):

1. Compiler: Install a Fortran compiler like GNU Fortran (gfortran).

2. Write Code: Create a `.f90` file and write a simple Fortran program.

```fortran
    PROGRAM HelloWorld
    WRITE(*,*) 'Hello, World!'
    END PROGRAM HelloWorld
```

3. Compile and Run: Use the terminal and run `gfortran filename.f90 -o HelloWorld && ./HelloWorld`.

4. Explore Scientific Computing: Fortran is widely used in scientific and numerical computing. Explore Fortran for its strengths in these domains.

Happy   coding   with   Fortran!

29

Lisp

To use Lisp (number 29 in the list of programming languages):

1. Environment: Set up a Lisp environment, such as Common Lisp or Scheme.

2. Write Code: Create a `.lisp` file and write a simple Lisp program.

```lisp
(format t "Hello, World!")
```

3. Run Code: Load and execute the Lisp file in your chosen Lisp environment.

4. Explore Functional Programming: Lisp is a functional programming language. Explore Lisp's powerful features like macros and higher-order functions.

Happy   coding   with   Lisp!

30

Prolog

To use Prolog (number 30 in the list of programming languages):

1. Prolog Interpreter: Install a Prolog interpreter like SWI-Prolog or GNU Prolog.

2. Write Code: Create a `.pl` file and write a simple Prolog program.

```prolog
greet :-
write('Hello, World!'),
nl.
```

3. Run Code: Use the Prolog interpreter and consult your file.

4. Explore Logic Programming: Prolog is a logic programming language. Explore its unique paradigm and use it for knowledge representation and rule-based systems.

Happy coding with Prolog!

www.ingramcontent.com/pod-product-compliance
Lightning Source LLC
Chambersburg PA
CBHW050050260726
48658CB00005B/187/9